— Animal Trackers —

TRACKING ANIMAL
IDENTITY

Tom Jackson

raintree

a Capstone company — publishers for children

Raintree is an imprint of Capstone Global Library Limited, a company incorporated in
England and Wales having its registered office at 7 Pilgrim Street, London EC4V 6LB
Registered company number 6695582

www.raintree.co.uk
myorders@raintree.co.uk

ISBN: 978-1-4747-0233-1

For Brown Bear Books Ltd:
Text: Tom Jackson
Designer: Lynne Lennon
Design Manager: Keith Davis
Editorial Director: Lindsey Lowe
Children's Publisher: Anne O'Daly
Picture Manager: Sophie Mortimer
Production Director: Alastair Gourlay

British Library Cataloguing in Publication Data
A full catalogue record for this book is available from the British Library.

Acknowledgements
t=top, c=centre, b=bottom, l=left, r=right

Front cover: Flip Nicklin/Minden/FLPA
1, ©Ryan Ladbrook/Shutterstock; 4, ©Andre Anita/Shutterstock; 5, ©Dieter Hawlan/Shutterstock; 6, ©Eon Alers/Shutterstock;
7t, ©Stefanie van der Vinden /Shutterstock; 7b, ©Gracious Tiger/Shutterstock; 8, ©Lightpoet/Shutterstock; 9, ©Tomatito/
Shutterstock; 10, ©John Downer/NaturePL; 11tl, ©Sylines/Shutterstock; 11tr, ©Igor Sokolov/Shutterstock; 11b, ©YK/
Shutterstock; 12, ©Ryan Ladbrook/Shutterstock; 13, ©Celiafoto/Shutterstock; 14, ©Dennis W. Donohue/Shutterstock; 14-15,
©Tom Reichner/Shutterstock; 15, ©StevenRussellSmithPhotos/Shutterstock; 16, ©TessarTheTegu/Shutterstock; 17, ©Anton
Ivanov/Shutterstock; 18, ©Gerard Soury/OSF/Getty Images; 19t, ©Matt9122/Shutterstock; 19b, ©Isoperla; 20-21t, ©Purestock/
Thinkstock; 20-21b, ©Nature Conservancy; 22, ©Isak5/Shutterstock; 23, ©Ipatov/Shutterstock; 24t, ©fotorince/Shutterstock; 24b,
©Jubal Harshaw /Shutterstock; 25, ©Jason Reed/Reuters/Corbis; 26cl, ©Corey Ford/Thinkstock; 26b, ©501room/Thinkstock;
27tl, ©Alice Photo/iStock/Thinkstock; 27tr, ©Albin/iStock/Thinkstock; 28, ©Sergey Nivens/Shutterstock.

All Artworks © Brown Bear Books Ltd
Brown Bear Books has made every attempt to contact the copyright holder.
If anyone has any information please contact licensing@brownbearbooks.co.uk.

Some words are shown in bold, **like this**. You can find out
what they mean by looking at the glossary.

Printed in China
19 18 17 16 15
10 9 8 7 6 5 4 3 2 1

CONTENTS

WHY WE TRACK ANIMAL IDENTITY

Every animal belongs to a group called a **species**. Scientists have discovered more than a million species so far. Scientists believe that there are millions more still to be identified. Technology can help us to find and understand new species.

Different types, or subspecies, of tiger live in Asia. All need protecting. To take care of tigers scientists have to be able to tell each type apart.

OUT OF SIGHT

It is not easy to know which species an animal belongs to. Many species are very rare or they live in places where few people live. Others are good at hiding and are rarely seen by people. There may be species that have never been seen by anyone.

This giant octopus lives in the deep waters of the Pacific Ocean. It lives too far down for most divers to visit. People only know they are there because octopuses are sometimes hauled up in fishing nets.

STUDYING SPECIES

The scientists who organise animals into different species are called **taxonomists**. They study each animal carefully, looking at its body features, such as its colours and size. They also consider what the animal eats and where it lives. If scientists find an animal with a unique set of characteristics, they will call it a new species. The most important feature of a species is that its members will breed with each other. They cannot breed with a member of another species.

Scientists use technology to identify which species an animal belongs to. Technology can also discover new, previously unknown species.

FACT: A quarter of all species on Earth are different types of beetles!

TAKING A LOOK

The simplest way to identify animals is to use your eyes. It takes practice, but you can learn to recognise different species just by looking. Books called field guides are useful. They are filled with information about identifying species.

Experts can identify a species from the signs it leaves behind. This footprint was left by an African lion.

BECOME AN EXPERT

Experts have to learn to identify the species they see in the wild. Make an expedition into the countryside and make a record of the animals you see. Soon the common species will become easy to identify.

A safari jeep passes two warthogs in Africa. The best way to see a lot of different species is to travel long distances through an area.

WHAT TO LOOK FOR

Many species can be identified by the way they look. However, some are so similar people need to use other techniques. **Biologists** develop identification guides called keys. These guides help them to work out what species they have seen. A key works by asking questions about the animal: how many legs does it have? Does it have horns? These simple questions help make clear what type of animal it is. To make a final identification, it is useful to check against the pictures in a field guide. For example, the key shows that you are looking at a type of cricket. Look up crickets in the field guide and try to find the picture that best matches the cricket you have seen. Identification complete!

Setting up feeders is a good way to see what bird species are in an area. This male northern cardinal has come to eat some of the seeds.

7

LOOKING CLOSER

Technology that helps you see further and closer is useful for spotting animals in the wild. Telescopes and binoculars are used to see animals that are far away. Microscopes show features that are too small to see with the eye alone.

This wildlife spotter has camouflaged himself and his powerful camera so that he does not disturb the animals in the area.

SEEING INTO THE DISTANCE

Most animals are much better at spotting people than people are at spotting them. As a result, animals run away when people get near. Other animals – like big cats and bears – are just too dangerous for people to get very close to.

Telescopes, binoculars and even camera lenses are used to watch shy creatures from a safe distance. These devices collect the light coming from a distant object and **magnify** the image of that object so it looks like it is much closer. An animal that is too far away to see with the **naked eye** becomes big enough to observe in detail.

FINE DETAILS

Microscopes take the light coming from a tiny part of an object that is too small to be seen clearly with the naked eye. Lenses inside the microscope magnify an image of that object. Nine out of every ten animal species is an insect, spider, worm or other **invertebrate**. Most are so small they can only be properly identified using a microscope.

A microscope reveals the detailed features on the head of a fly. A close look such as this helps to identify the exact species.

FACT: If a person had the eyesight of an eagle he or she could read this book from the other side of the room.

CAMERA TRAP

The most shy animals can be difficult to observe in the wild. A wildlife expert might have to wait many days to spot them. Instead scientists use "traps" to get a close look.

HIDDEN CAMERAS

The type of traps they use do not harm the animal. They do not even touch it. A camera trap is set up in a spot where scientists know the target animals live. It takes a picture, capturing a moment in the animal's life when it is behaving naturally. The camera is normally camouflaged. Even if it is not disguised, the animals soon get used to it and ignore it after a while.

This camera trap is disguised as a pile of rocks. It is remote controlled so it can be driven to new locations.

TECHNOLOGY: Inside a camera trap

Camera traps use a digital camera (left) and a motion sensor (right) like the ones fitted in burglar alarms. When the sensor detects a movement, the camera takes a picture.

TARGET ANIMALS

Camera traps are used to take pictures of the world's rarest animals. A camera trap took pictures of a clouded leopard that lives in Borneo and Sumatra. The photos showed that the cat was in fact a separate species from the clouded leopards that live on the Asian mainland.

Camera traps can also capture rare moments in an animal's life. These help identify animals in the future. For example, traps set around the den of a **pregnant** animal can take pictures of the young when they are born. These pictures show people what the baby animals look like when very young.

Fox cubs in the wild are rarely seen by people, but a camera trap can take their picture without scaring the cubs away.

TRACKS AND SIGNS

Many animals leave behind signs at places they have been. Some signs, such as a spider's web or deer's footprints, are left by animal activity. Some animals leave special signs to show other animals they are in the area.

WATER HUNTER

The river otter is difficult to spot in the wild, but it leaves its mark. Different species of river otter live in different parts of the world, but they all leave similar tracks and signs behind.

TRACKS AND SLIDES

River otters hunt for fish and other prey in water but come on to land to rest. The most obvious signs that otters create are called slides. These are the places that the otter uses to climb in and out of the water. Slides are normally on steep banks.

Otters slip under the water whenever people come near so it is rare to see one. However, the tracks and other signs the otters leave are easier to find.

WOW!

Even extinct animals leave tracks. These footprints on the right were made by a dinosaur walking through mud. When the mud turned to stone, the prints remained. The oldest dinosaur footprints ever found are in Poland and were made 250 million years ago. Scientists can identify dinosaurs by their footprints. The tracks also show how heavy the dinosaur was and how fast it moved.

These fossil prints have been filled with water to make them easier to see.

The otter's body leaves an **impression** in the mud as it slides into the water. It flattens any plants growing there. The soft soil around a slide is also a good place to look for otter footprints.

SCENT MARKS

Otters advertise their presence to other animals with scent marks called spraints. These are small lumps of dung mixed with smelly jelly. They are a sign that an otter is nearby. The otter leaves the spraint on a rock or other place that is easy to see. The spraints mark the otter's **territory**. Their smell warns other otters not to come too near.

JOIN IN

Finding river otters

River otters were once hunted for their fur and they are much less common than they used to be. However, you may see signs of one near a river. They prefer quiet, clean waterways in forested areas, but they also live on beaches. Search for guides to otter tracks and signs online at organisations such as these:

The Mammal Society
Devon Biodiversity Records Centre (DBRC)

woodpecker Marks

woodpeckers are common birds in forests around the world. They are more often heard than seen but can be identified from the damage they cause.

Woodpeckers are famous for drilling into wood. Their high-speed pecking makes a loud noise that can be heard around the forest. Each species creates a particular type of damage to trees and other wooden objects.

Insect diggers

Most woodpeckers are insect eaters. They use their long, chisel-shaped beaks to dig out insect **larvae** that live in wood. The woodpeckers may tap the wood, listening for hollow sounds. That tells them that a grub is burrowing around inside. The bird drills into the wood with its beak and gets at the prey using its long tongue. Different species feed in specialised ways. Some look for dead wood. Others dig into living tree trunks. Woodpeckers also rip off bark to get at the bugs living underneath. All this activity leaves tell-tale marks.

Acorn woodpecker

As their name suggests, North American acorn woodpeckers eat acorns, which are the nuts of oak trees. They store the nuts in "granaries", placing them in holes pecked into dead wood.

Look-alikes

The hairy woodpecker and downy woodpecker look very similar. Both species live in North America. The downy woodpecker (right) is smaller and has a shorter beak.

Surveying

Woodpeckers migrate south from places with very cold winters but stay all year in warmer areas. They are most active in spring and summer when they are digging nests and feeding young. This is the best time to look for woodpecker damage. Much of it will be high above the ground. You will need binoculars to spot it.

Nest holes

As well as pecking holes for feeding, woodpeckers also dig larger chambers for nests. The nest hole takes about a month to dig and is lined with wood chips.

The downy woodpecker pecks small holes and scrapes off bark.

The hairy woodpecker strips the bark off trees.

The pileated woodpecker digs big holes in tree trunks.

The sapsucker drills small holes in straight lines.

LISTENING FOR SOUNDS

Even if you cannot see an animal you might be able to hear it. Sound is used by animals to communicate. Each species can be identified by its calls.

MAKING NOISES

Animals make calls in two ways. First, sounds such as birdsong and frog croaks are made by **vocal cords** in the throat. When the animal blows air through them, the cords vibrate and produce musical tones.

Male frogs attract mates with croaks. The throat is inflated with air, and the stretched skin vibrates like a drum skin, making the croaks louder.

FACT: Blue whale calls are louder than jet engines and carry for up to 800 kilometres (500 miles).

Second, most insect calls, such as the chirrup of a cricket, are made by **stridulation**. Legs and wings are rubbed together to make clicking sounds.

WHY CALL AT ALL?

Calls are meant to advertise an animal's presence. There are two main reasons for doing this. First, the animal calls to tell other members of the species to stay out of its territory. Second, they are calling to attract a mate. To do both of these things, each species produces a unique pattern of sounds. Scientists can use the sounds to identify the species.

WOW!

The call of the greater bulldog bat of South America is as loud as a gunshot (only it is too high pitched for human ears to pick up). Australia's green grocer cicada is louder than a lawnmower. It makes calls by vibrating its body 300 times a second. A lion's roar is quiet by comparison. It is only as loud as a drum, but its low rumble can travel for 8 kilometres (5 miles).

Howler monkeys produce loud calls in the early morning. The large throat pouch makes the call louder.

RECORDING CALLS

The human ear cannot pick up many animal calls. They are too low or too high pitched. The calls that can be heard are often very complex. To understand them better, scientists record the calls so they can study them in detail.

A hydrophone (an underwater microphone) is used to pick up whale calls.

MAKING WAVES

Sound is a wave that travels through the air or water. High-pitched sounds, like a squeak, are made of sound waves that have a high frequency. That means the wave rises and falls very quickly. Low-pitched sounds, like a roar or growl, have a low frequency.

PC 3799 AY 18   RIVER

FACT: A dolphin can knock out a fish with a targeted burst of high-pitched sound.

MAKING RECORDS

A recording device converts the vibrations in the air or in the water into an electrical signal that can be stored and played back. The human ear can only pick up a small range of frequencies, but microphones can detect any sound. A recording can be sped up or slowed down to a pitch that people can hear. In this way, scientists have found that elephants produce deep rumbling calls, and dolphins make high-pitched squeaks and clicks. A computer analyses the recording and breaks it up into sections. This helps scientists work out what the call is for.

Dolphins use high-pitched whistles and clicks to communicate and to locate prey.

The app gives a list of possible matches of each call and can normally identify the right bird.

JOIN IN

Identifying bird calls

You can identify a bird call with a smartphone app. The device records the call and then compares the sound against a database of calls. Search for apps online, such as this one:

Bird Song ID (Isoperla)

Search online for this organisation to listen to an audio library of bird calls:

RSPB Bird Guide

19

Identifying Bats

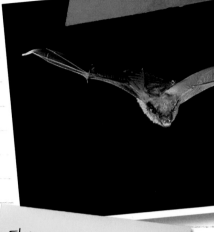

Bats are hard to see in the dark, but they can be identified by their high-pitched calls.

Most bats hunt in the dark. Instead of using their eyes to find prey, they use echolocation. They send out high-pitched calls that echo off objects around them. The bats listen for the echoes and use them to create a picture of their surroundings.

Flying mammals

Bats are the only type of **mammal** that can fly. The wings are not made from feathers like a bird's. Instead they are flaps of skin stretched over long finger bones.

Picturing sound

Every species of bat produces a unique echolocation call. They also communicate with each other with a range of sounds. Bat calls are almost always too high pitched to hear, so scientists use specialist recording equipment to study them. The calls are complex, and the best way to understand them is to make them into a sonogram (right). This is a picture of the sound, which shows all the different tones in the call. As well as identifying the species of bat, a sonogram shows scientists how the echolocation system works.

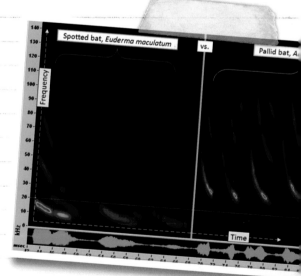

Spotted bat, *Euderma maculatum*   vs.   Pallid bat, A...

Hidden species

Call analysis has found that the pipistrelle bat is actually two species, the common pipistrelle and soprano pipistrelle. The bats of both species look just the same but each species uses distinct calls to find prey and communicate.

Echolocation calls

Scientists pick up the calls of a bat with a special detector. The detector converts the calls into sounds that humans can hear. The pitch of the call is used to identify the species.

JOIN IN

Bat detectives

Try your hand at identifying bats by their calls. This website has a collection of recorded sounds and sonograms. Search online for this organisation to learn about sonograms:

Bat Conservation Trust

Train yourself to identify a bat from its sound and find out more about how to find and record bats yourself.

2 A bat uses the echo to find its way to the moth.

1 The bat's call (yellow) makes an echo (red) when it hits the moth.

3 The detector picks up the bat's loud call and converts it into a sound that humans can hear (green).

allidous

The grey line indicates the high end frequency limit of human hearing, about 20 kHz. Rarely can a person hear frequencies higher than this.

DNA
AND CHEMICALS

It is possible to identify a species from a piece of its body. This could be a bone from a skeleton, a feather or a sample of blood. All of these contain DNA and other chemicals that can be used to identify the species.

Every animal has a unique genetic fingerprint, but members of the same species will have very similar ones.

DNA CODE

The term DNA is short for deoxyribonucleic acid. This is a complicated chain-like chemical that is found in every cell of a body. The structure of the DNA carries coded instructions called genes. The genes are used to organise how a body grows.

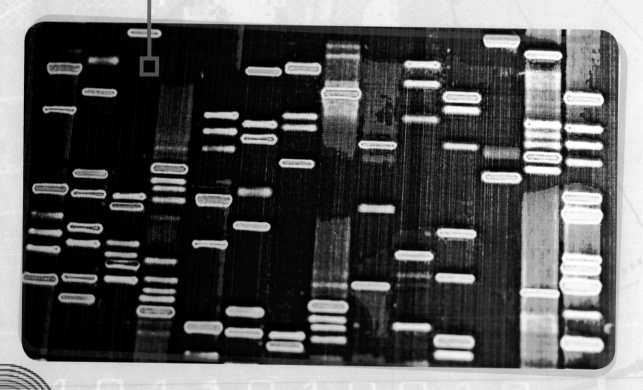

A species' complete set of genes is called its genome. One way of studying a genome is to make a genetic fingerprint. This turns the DNA into a unique pattern of bands, which can be used to identify a species.

OTHER CHEMICALS

Studying DNA is a long and complicated process. It is often easier to use other chemicals to identify a species. Blood cells are covered in substances called **antigens**, which can help to identify an animal. The chemicals in hair, skin and muscle show what an animal has been eating and also helps to identify its species.

A liger has pale stripes like a tiger and a small mane like a lion.

WOW!

A hybrid is an animal with parents belonging to two related species. A mule is a hybrid of a donkey and horse, while a liger (left) has a tiger and lion as parents. Hybrid animals have DNA from two species, but that does not make them a new species. Most hybrid animals are unable to have young.

FACT: An offspring of a male zebra and a female donkey is called a zonkey!

Using Fur

High-tech analysis techniques can identify a species from a single strand of hair.

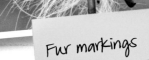

The only animals to have true hairs are mammals. Most mammal species have a distinctive pattern on their fur, often for **camouflage**. The fur pattern is one of the ways mammals can be identified, but the hairs themselves contain unique information.

Hair structure

Mammal hair is made from **keratin**. This is the same chemical that is found in fingernails, horns, bird feathers and reptile scales. The colour of a hair comes from a mixture of chemicals called pigments. There are three main pigments. Darker hair has three pigments. Light hairs, such as yellow and red colours, have one or two. The palest hair – white – has no pigment at all. If there is enough fur to show a pattern, it may be possible to identify a species. DNA **analysis** and other techniques can be used to identify a species from just one hair.

Fur markings

Animal hairs can be seen tangled on thorns or other sharp objects. Some animals, such as bears and wildcats, leave patches of fur to mark out their territory.

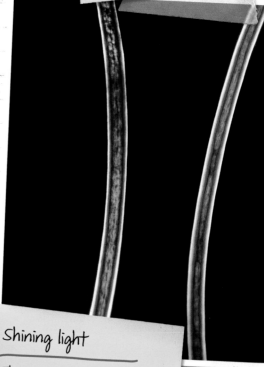

Shining light

The mix of pigments in a hair make it reflect light in a particular way. This can be examined with special microscopes, which allow scientists to compare the hairs of different species.

chemical analysis

A mass spectrometer can tell scientists which chemicals are in a mixture. Analysing the hair of an unknown animal this way can reveal what it has eaten recently and where it might have been living.

2 Scientists analyse the hairs to see if they belong to a new species ...

3 ... but the hairs are from common forest animals.

Looking for Bigfoot!

Some people believe that ape-like creatures live in the forests of North America. They call the animal Bigfoot. Several people claim to have found samples of Bigfoot fur, but DNA analysis of the hairs always shows that they belong to a known animal.

1 A "Bigfoot" fur sample is found.

FOSSILS

There are many more **extinct** species than species living today. However, scientists can identify many of these long-gone animals from the fossils left behind.

WHAT ARE FOSSILS?

The most familiar fossils are rocks in the shape of bones and shells. Fossils like these form when the animal is buried suddenly. The soft body parts rot away, but the hard parts remain. Over millions of years, the bone and shell is washed away and replaced with rock-like minerals. However, the original shape can still be seen.

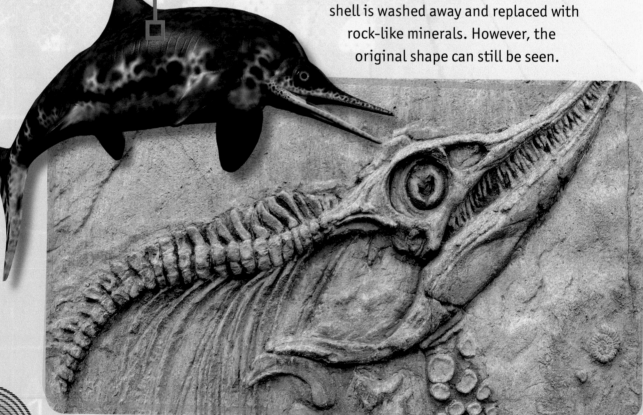

This fossil is an ichthyosaur, a large marine reptile that looked like a fish or dolphin. Scientists use fossils to reconstruct what the living animal might have looked like.

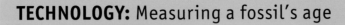

TECHNOLOGY: Measuring a fossil's age

This giant shellfish is about 200 million years old. Scientists can work out the age of a fossil by measuring its natural **radioactivity** with a detector. The rock of older fossils has lower levels of certain types of radioactivity than are found in younger ones.

STUDYING FOSSILS

Some fossilised animals are complete skeletons, and it is easier to identify the species. Other fossils are just a few body parts, such as a tooth or a leg bone. Fossil experts are known as **palaeontologists**. To identify what kind of animal a fossil once belonged to, experts compare it with the body parts of better-known fossils and living species. They also scan fossils with **X-rays** to look at internal structures. Making 3D computer scans of each specimen gives a more detailed view.

OTHER SIGNS

Fossils do not only show body parts. There are fossil nests, eggs, footprints and even fossilised dung. Palaeontologists classify these kinds of fossils separately from the actual animals that left them behind. However, these fossils are still useful for showing how ancient species once lived.

THE FUTURE

As scientists are able to describe more species, new high-tech techniques will be needed to make their job easier. These might include using scents to track animals in the wild or looking for invisible light that reflects off animals in different ways.

IN THE FIELD

Most high-technology techniques have to be carried out in the **laboratory.** In the future, the machines used will get small enough to carry around so scientists can take them to where the animals are. There are already portable machines that can analyse DNA. One day, it may be possible to identify species from blood or other samples taken anywhere in the world.

The genes of every species are being recorded in a huge database. In future a scientist could identify a species by searching through this genetic information in the same way we search the Internet today.

FACT: Dogs recognise each other by smell. Their noses are 10,000 times more sensitive than a human's.

SNIFFING OUT

It is common for animals to have an identifying smell. This is how many of them communicate with each other, attract mates or mark a territory. A human nose cannot detect most of the smells but odour-sensitive devices can. For this type of technology to work, researchers will need to record the scents of different species. Then the sniffing gadget could pick up the tell-tale smells in the wild.

INVISIBLE LIGHT

Sunlight contains **ultraviolet** (UV) rays. Human eyes cannot see these rays but many animals can. The world looks very different to them. Perhaps UV-sensitive cameras will help scientists to identify new species in the future.

This is what a starling looks like to another starling. The UV light gives it much brighter colours than when it is looked at in normal sunlight.

29

GLOSSARY

analysis detailed study of something by breaking it down into simpler parts

antigens chemical on a living cell that identifies it as belonging to the body

biologist scientist who studies plants, animals and other living things

camouflage disguise that blends in with the surroundings

extinct no longer existing

impression mark made in a soft surface, such as mud

invertebrate animal without bones or a spine

keratin flexible protein. It waterproofs the skin and makes body coverings like hair and feathers.

laboratory work space used by scientists to carry out research

larvae young forms of certain insects. A larva is very different from the adult form. Larvae include caterpillars, the young form of butterflies.

magnify make something appear bigger than it really is

mammal animal that grows hairs and feeds its young on milk

naked eye using the eye without any device to help vision

palaeontologist expert in fossils and ancient, extinct life forms

pregnant having a baby or babies developing inside the body

radioactivity natural process in which certain materials break apart and release radiation

species group of animals that can breed with each other

stridulation making noises by rubbing body parts together

taxonomist scientist who organises animals and other life forms into species and larger groupings

territory in terms of biology, this is an area controlled by an animal

ultraviolet high-energy light that human eyes cannot see

vocal cord flap of skin in the throat that vibrates to make a sound wave

X-rays invisible rays that can travel through solid objects and can be used to make images of the inside of things

READ MORE

Animals Up Close. Igor Siwanowicz. London: Dorling Kindersley, 2010.

Big RSPB Birdwatch: Get to know the birds outside your window. David Chandler. London: Bloomsbury, 2011.

Mammals (Classifying Animals). Sarah Wilkes. London: Wayland, 2007.

RSPB Guide to Nature Watching. Mark Boyd. London: Bloomsbury, 2013.

The Bat Scientists (Scientists in the Field). Mary Kay Carson. New York: Houghton Mifflin, 2010.

Wild Tracks: A guide to nature's footprints. Jim Arnosky. New York: Sterling, 2008.

INTERNET SITES

The Mammal Society
How to tell if are otters are living nearby.
www.mammal.org.uk/
mawsespeciesguides/otter-3

Devon Biodiversity Records Centre
How otter surveys are carried out.
www.dbrc.org.uk

Bird Song ID (Isoperla)
www.isoperla.co.uk/Birdid.html

RSPB Bird Guide
An audio guide to bird songs and calls.
www.rspb.org.uk/discoverandenjoynature/
discoverandlearn/birdguide

Bat Conservation Trust
Information on identifying Britain's different bats.
bats.www.bats.org.uk/pages/all_about_
bats.html

INDEX